CULTURAL CONTRIBUTIONS FROM
EAST ASIA

FIREWORKS, TEA, AND MORE

GREAT CULTURES,
GREAT IDEAS

MADELINE TYLER

PowerKiDS
press

Published in 2019 by The Rosen Publishing Group, Inc.
29 East 21st Street, New York, NY 10010

Cataloging-in-Publication Data

Names: Tyler, Madeline.
Title: Cultural contributions from East Asia: fireworks, tea, and more / Madeline Tyler.
Description: New York : PowerKids Press, 2019. l Series: Great cultures, great ideas l Includes glossary and index.
Identifiers: LCCN ISBN 9781538338186 (pbk.) l ISBN 9781538338179 (library bound) l ISBN 9781538338193 (6 pack)
Subjects: LCSH: East Asia--Civilization--Juvenile literature. l East Asia--Social life and customs--Juvenile literature. l
Inventions--Asia--History--Juvenile literature.
Classification: LCC DS509.3 T954 2019 l DDC 951--dc23

Written by: Madeline Tyler
Edited by: Holly Duhig
Designed by: Gareth Liddington

Photo credits
Abbreviations: l-left, r-right, b-bottom, t-top, c-center, m-middle.

Front Cover – Ociacia, ajt, isak55, Heactor Sanchez, paseven, Jemastock, langdu, Nisakorn Neera, Lemau Studio, interstid, gresei,
2 - Arun no sekai, 4 - stocker1970, Jakkarin Apikornrat, Creative-Touch, AJP, Sirisak Chantorn, Memory Stockphoto, piyaphong,
5 - AJ Frames, DisobeyAr, Sata Production, Jennifer Lam, Kamil Macniak, 6 - Magdanatka, I am Corona, hxdyl, 7 - sebasnoo, Heath Doman,
Maximumvector, charnsitr, 8 - Globe Turner, Gil C, Picsfive, Loveshop, 10 - fotohunter, Patra.K, 11 - Chinaview, Alik Mulikov, 12 - David Franklin,
qvist, poonsap, 13 - Subbotina Anna, L.F, Mike Pond, 14 - Liu zishan, GOLFX, Alex Staroseltsev, 15 - MilanB, Early Spring, Andrey_Kuzmin,
16 - antpkr, Mohd KhairilX, Mega Pixel, 17 - koosen, zzcapture, PHOTOCREO Michal Bednarek, 18 - ShutterOK, KPG_Payless,
19 - nunosilvaphotography, Sakarin Sawasdinaka, Daiquiri, taa22, 20 - maki watanabe, Bobnevv, Ronnachai Palas, eduardo woo
21 - ssguy, Navigator84, Matthias93, wikimedia, Hatsukari715, LSDSL, 22 - Yuravector, 23 - Pil56, tanyalmera, liza54500,
24 - tongcom photographer, 25 - Sapann Desgn, VikaSuh, Visual Generation, 26 - Arcansel, flickr, wikimedia, DennisM2, Samsung,
sorawich pakkase, 27 - James Steidi, Africa Studio, vladwel, 28 - Bignai, Vitaphoto.ru, Suradech Prapairat, yoruhana, Eva Rinaldi,
29 - SaMBa, JAITY, 30 - dikobraziy, vectorfusionart.

Images are courtesy of Shutterstock.com. With thanks to Getty Images, Thinkstock Photo and iStockphoto.

Manufactured in the United States of America

CPSIA Compliance Information: Batch #CSPK18: For Further Information contact
Rosen Publishing, New York, New York at 1-800-237-9932.

CONTENTS

Words that look like **this** are explained in the glossary on page 31.

WHAT IS CULTURE?

If you were to travel around the world, visiting lots of countries on the way, you would probably notice that certain things around you would not be the same as they are at home. The countries and places you visit, and the people you meet, would have different languages, customs, and ways of doing things. The food might be different, the way people dress might be different, and even the laws and rules might be different to what you know at home. All of these things, when put together, make up what we call the culture of a place.

A HOUSE IN CHINA MIGHT LOOK VERY DIFFERENT THAN ONE IN THE UK!

WHAT MAKES UP A CULTURE?

Shared ideas and traditions that make up a culture can include:

LAWS	HOLIDAYS
FOOD	FAMILIES
LEADERS	SCHOOLS
SYMBOLS	SPECIAL BUILDINGS
BELIEFS	HOSPITALS
CEREMONIES	ENTERTAINMENT

A culture can also be shared by a group of people who might not live near each other, but who share a way of life. People who like the same music or hobbies can share a culture. People who all belong to the same religion can be said to share a culture, no matter where they live.

BEAUTIFUL HENNA TATTOOS ARE PART OF INDIAN CULTURE. MANY INDIAN BRIDES AROUND THE WORLD PRACTICE THIS CULTURAL TRADITION.

Our culture is a big part of our identity. Having a distinctive culture is what makes places or people unique. Knowing you belong to a particular culture is a good feeling. It's nice to share our culture with other people. If we are in a culture we recognize, we understand what to do or how to act.

DIFFERENT CULTURES GREET EACH OTHER IN DIFFERENT WAYS - A HANDSHAKE, A BOW, OR EVEN A KISS!

GLOBAL CULTURE

Even though every culture is different and unique, many cultures also have lots of things in common. We can learn a lot from other cultures, and share the things we know and like. In the past, when people started traveling to other cultures, they swapped and shared their food.

They shared traditions and knowledge, and people started to adopt things from other cultures into their own. For example, British people see drinking tea as part of their cultural identity—but tea is originally from China and is also an important part of Japanese culture.

AFTERNOON TEA, WITH CAKES AND SANDWICHES, IS A TRADITIONAL PART OF ENGLISH CULTURE.

IN JAPAN, THE TEA CEREMONY IS AN IMPORTANT CULTURAL RITUAL.

TEA WAS ORIGINALLY FROM CHINA AND ORIGINATED DURING THE SHANG DYNASTY.

It is also really interesting to explore other cultures and discover new and exciting ways of doing things! We can share our ideas and learn new things when cultures meet.

MY CULTURE, YOUR CULTURE, OUR CULTURE

Adopting ideas from other cultures can lead to really interesting results. Many cultures take inspiration from others and adapt and change their traditions and customs to make them their own. Putting two ideas from two different cultures together can produce new and exciting things. Did you know that a pizza in Italy will look very different from a pizza in the US? Italians introduced pizza, a traditional Italian dish, to the Americans living in the US. A traditional Italian pizza has a thin, crispy crust, and lots of tomato, but only a small amount of mozzarella cheese. An American pizza has a thick, fluffy base, is smothered in cheese, and can have lots of different toppings – meats, fish, even pineapple! Both cultures share a love for pizza, but each culture has their own way of doing things!

TRADITIONAL ITALIAN PIZZA

WHICH PIZZA DO YOU PREFER? ITALIAN, AMERICAN, OR MAYBE A SLICE OF EACH?

TRADITIONAL AMERICAN PIZZA

WHERE IS EAST ASIA?

East Asia is made up of several contries, including China, Japan, South Korea, Mongolia, and Taiwan. It is found in the Northern and Eastern **hemispheres**.

Mongolia

Capital city: Ulaanbaatar
Population: 2,756,000 people
Size: 604,600 square miles (1,565,906 sq km)
Currency: Mongolian togrog
Major religion(s): Buddhism, Islam, Christianity, **Shamanism**
Main language(s): Mongolian

China

Capital city: Beijing
Population: 1,200,000,000 people
Size: 3,705,000 square miles (9,595,905 sq km)
Currency: Renminbi (Yuan)
Major religion(s): Buddhism, Christianity, Islam, **Taoism**
Main language(s): Mandarin Chinese

CAN YOU SPOT WHERE
EAST ASIA IS?

Japan

Capital city: Tokyo
Population: 127,400,000 people
Size: 145,932 square miles
(377,962 sq km)
Currency: Yen
Major religion(s): Shintoism,
Buddhism
Main language(s): Japanese

South Korea

Capital city: Seoul
Population: 51,100,000 people
Size: 38,691 square miles
(100,210 sq km)
Currency: Won
Major religion(s): Buddhism,
Christianity
Main language(s): Korean

Taiwan

Capital city: Taipei
Population: 23,500,000 people
Size: 13,974 square miles
(36,192 sq km)
Currency: New Taiwan Dollar
Major religion(s): Taoism,
Buddhism, Christianity
Main language(s): Mandarin Chinese,
Min, Nan Chinese (Taiwanese), Hakka

FIREWORKS

Have you ever seen a fireworks display? Maybe it was at a wedding or a big celebration such as New Year's Eve? Fireworks are traditionally set off on the 4th of July to celebrate America's Independence Day. With their bright colors and loud explosions, it is easy to see why fireworks are a popular way to celebrate important events. In fact, they are so popular that around 14,000 fireworks displays light up American skies every year on the 4th of July.

FIREWORKS DISPLAY IN SAN FRANCISCO, CALIFORNIA

Fireworks might seem like quite a modern invention, but did you know they have been around for over 1,000 years and were invented in China? By the 9th century, the Chinese had already invented gunpowder, which explodes in a loud bang when it is lighted. They soon discovered that putting gunpowder inside bamboo shoots and throwing them on a fire made a loud blast. The firecracker was born.

The Chinese continued to experiment with these explosives, and making fireworks became a **profession**. By the 10th century, when the Song Dynasty ruled China, fireworks had become an important part of celebrations. The loud noises and bright explosions were thought to ward off evil spirits. Nowadays, fireworks are a traditional part of Chinese New Year celebrations.

THE ART OF MAKING FIREWORKS IS CALLED PYROTECHNICS.

The colorful fireworks we see today are made by mixing gunpowder with other substances. For example, green fireworks are made by mixing gunpowder with the **chemical** barium, and blue fireworks are made with a type of metal called copper.

SPARKLERS ARE DESIGNED TO BURN FOR A LONG TIME.

PRINTING AND PAPER

PAPER

Paper is something we come across every day. We use it to write on in school, and to make books, newspapers, and even money. This book is even made of paper! However, paper has not always been around. Before paper was invented, people used bones, bamboo, and even tortoise shells to write on. These materials were very heavy, so transporting them was extremely difficult, and they also took up a lot of space. Can you imagine writing your homework on a tortoise shell?

PAPER MONEY AND PLAYING CARDS WERE ALSO INVENTED IN CHINA!

CHINESE LANTERNS

Paper was invented over 2,000 years ago during the Han Dynasty in China. Dynasties are a line of people, like a royal family, who ruled over China at different points in history. The first types of paper were made using rags and tree bark. This produced paper that was coarse and thick and had an uneven texture, which made it quite bulky and difficult to write on.

PAPER LANTERNS ARE VERY POPULAR THROUGHOUT CHINA AND EAST ASIA. TRADITIONALLY, THEY SYMBOLIZE JOY, CELEBRATION, AND GOOD FORTUNE.

Later, it was discovered that using fibers from the bamboo plant and bark from a mulberry tree produced a different type of paper that was smoother and more transportable. This was made by mixing finely chopped mulberry bark with bamboo fibers, crushing it flat to press out all the moisture, and then letting it dry in the sun. These raw materials were cheap and could be readily found, meaning that large quantities of paper could now be produced at a low cost. This paper was a success and was soon used across China.

PRINTING

THIS IS WHAT BAMBOO LOOKS LIKE.

THESE ARE "MOVEABLE TYPE" CHARACTERS.

WOODBLOCK PRINTING

This cheap form of paper eventually led to the creation of different methods of printing. The first method to come about was woodblock printing. **Characters** were cut into a wooden block and then dipped in ink. The woodblock was pressed onto paper, leaving a print of the characters. Woodblock printing was a very slow and expensive process, so a faster and more **efficient** method was needed.

MOVEABLE TYPE PRINTING

Moveable type printing was created during the Song Dynasty to speed up the printing process. It rapidly spread across Asia and, later, around the whole world. Individual characters were carved onto pieces of clay, hardened, and then glued to an iron plate. The characters could be broken up and moved around to print different pages.

MAGNETIC COMPASSES

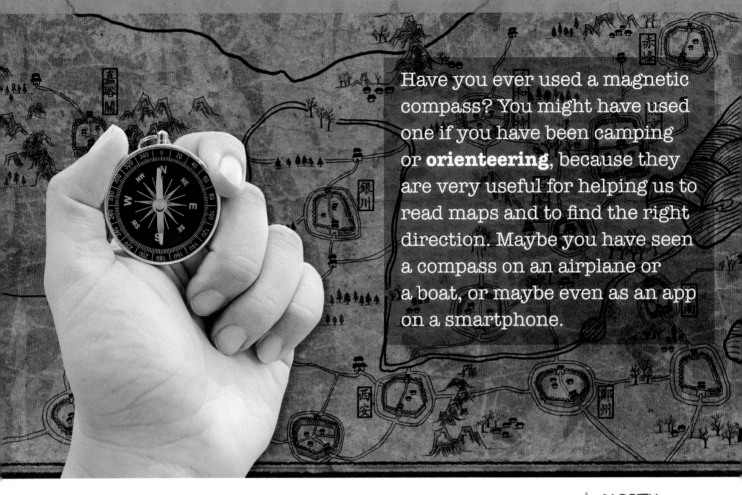

Have you ever used a magnetic compass? You might have used one if you have been camping or **orienteering**, because they are very useful for helping us to read maps and to find the right direction. Maybe you have seen a compass on an airplane or a boat, or maybe even as an app on a smartphone.

Magnetic compasses have changed a lot since they were first invented some time between the 11th and 12th century by the Chinese. The first magnetic compass was very simple and was made up of a magnetic needle attached to a piece of wood or cork that floated freely in a bowl of water. The magnetized needle would be attracted and repelled by the Earth's **magnetic field**, causing it to spin in the water!

THE CHINESE FIRST USED MAGNETIC COMPASSES TO ORGANIZE BUILDINGS AND OTHER THINGS ACCORDING TO FENG SHUI.

NORTH

SOUTH

THE EARTH IS ACTUALLY A GIANT MAGNET WITH MAGNETIC NORTH AND SOUTH POLES.

MAKE YOUR OWN MAGNETIC COMPASS!

YOU WILL NEED

- Bowl of water
- Needle
- Bar magnet
- Piece of wood or cork

THIS IS A BAR MAGNET.

METHOD

1. First you will need to magnetize your needle so that it acts like the magnetic needle of a compass. You can do this by rubbing a bar magnet along it. Slide the "N" (North) end of the bar magnet along the needle, from one end to the other. Repeat 50 times (or until your hands hurt!).
2. Now turn the needle upside down and use the "S" (South) end of the magnet to rub the needle from the bottom to the top. Repeat this 50 times.
3. Carefully place the needle on the bit of wood or cork and let them float on the water.
4. Watch to see your needle spin to point north!

TOOTHBRUSHES

Keeping our teeth clean is very important, and we should brush our teeth twice a day. Nowadays, toothbrushes are made from plastic and a material called nylon. It is even possible to buy electric or sonic toothbrushes. But how did people brush their teeth hundreds of years ago? Before toothbrushes, the Chinese used "chewing sticks" made from **aromatic** trees and plants. These chewing sticks were also used in Africa, the Middle East, and India. The first bristle toothbrushes were invented around 600 years ago during the Ming Dynasty and were made by sticking coarse **hog's hair** into either bamboo or bone. The hog's hair was very wiry and, although good at cleaning, may have damaged the teeth by removing some of the **enamel**!

CHEWING STICK

MODERN TOOTHBRUSH

THE AVERAGE PERSON USES 27 ROLLS OF TOILET PAPER EVERY YEAR!

TOILET PAPER

Can you imagine living in a world without toilet paper? Before the Chinese invented it around 1,200 years ago during the Tang Dynasty, many people had to make do with leaves and fabrics like wool. For many years, toilet paper was not actually paper at all, but instead was made from huge sheets of soft fabric! This was expensive, so only the **emperors** and their family could use it in their homes.

UMBRELLAS

Umbrellas have been used in China for almost 2,000 years, but they were originally used for protecting people from the sun and were called sun parasols. Chinese emperors wanted something to provide shade for when they travelled in their carriages and a sun parasol did just that. China is very hot and sunny, so having sun parasols was useful for keeping cool. One important feature of umbrellas is that they can fold down, making them easy to transport and store. The folding umbrella was invented around 1,700 years ago during the Cao Wei Dynasty.

The top of the umbrella was originally made from silk, until paper was later used. Treating the silk (or paper) with wax made the umbrella waterproof.

The handle and frame were made from bamboo or mulberry tree bark.

ONLY MEMBERS OF THE IMPERIAL FAMILY COULD USE YELLOW AND RED UMBRELLAS. ORDINARY PEOPLE HAD TO USE BLUE.

UMBRELLAS WERE ONCE A SYMBOL OF POWER AND WEALTH. VERY HIGH-STATUS PEOPLE HAD BIG UMBRELLAS, WHICH NEEDED LOTS OF PEOPLE TO CARRY THEM.

TEA

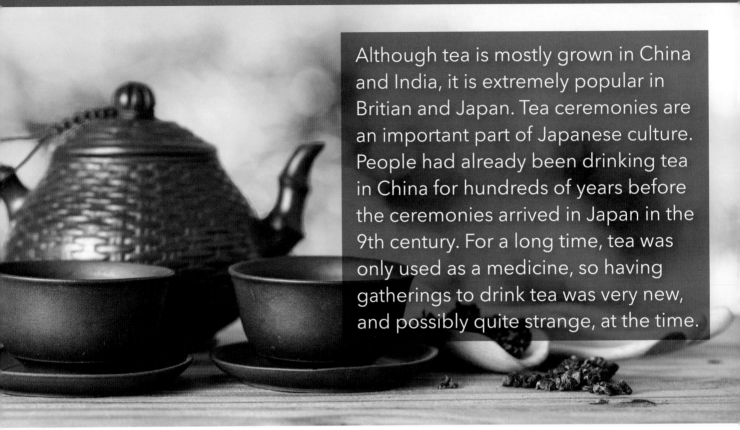

Although tea is mostly grown in China and India, it is extremely popular in Britian and Japan. Tea ceremonies are an important part of Japanese culture. People had already been drinking tea in China for hundreds of years before the ceremonies arrived in Japan in the 9th century. For a long time, tea was only used as a medicine, so having gatherings to drink tea was very new, and possibly quite strange, at the time.

Tea ceremonies are like a form of **meditation**, and relaxation is a very important part of the ceremonies. Rituals are another important element. Each ritual, like the preparation of the matcha tea, is led by the tea host and is seen as an art. It is very difficult to become a tea host—it takes more than ten years. This is because a person must study things like **philosophy**, art, and **calligraphy**, and learn the many tea preparations.

INNER HARMONY, TRANQUILITY, PURITY, AND RESPECT ARE KEY TO THE TEA CEREMONIES.

IN JAPANESE, THE CEREMONY IS CALLED SADO (茶道).

WELCOME TO THE TEA CEREMONY!

KONNICHIWA!
こんにちわ!

Welcome to Japan and welcome to the tea ceremony. Come inside and we can begin...

THIS IS MATCHA TEA IN A TEA BOWL.

1. You follow your host through the garden and wash your hands to cleanse.
2. You bow to pass through a very small door, showing respect.
3. You watch as the host kneels on a cushion and slowly cleans their tools. While this happens, a kettle of water is boiling on a stove.
4. The host inspects, folds, and unfolds a silk cloth (fukusa). They use the silk cloth to pick up the hot kettle.
5. Matcha and hot water are whisked together in a bowl.
6. The host passes the bowl to the first guest—pay close attention because it is your turn next!
7. The first guest turns the bowl around and takes a sip. They wipe it and pass it to you.
8. The tea is quite bitter, so the host serves some wagashi candies.
9. The bowl passes around all the guests until it reaches the host.

TECHNOLOGY

VIDEO GAMES

Playing video games is very popular. Almost half of all homes in the US own a gaming console that is used regularly. These consoles might be a Sony PlayStation, a Nintendo Wii, or a Nintendo Switch. Do you play video or computer games at home? PlayStation was invented by Ken Kutaragi, and Nintendo was founded by Fusajiro Yamauchi. What do these two people have in common? They are both Japanese!

NINTENDO WAS FOUNDED IN 1889. IT USED TO MAKE PLAYING CARDS LIKE THESE!

POKÉMON GO IS A POPULAR MOBILE PHONE GAME.

Sony and Nintendo are Japanese companies, but their games and consoles are now sold all over the world. Japan has had a huge influence on worldwide gaming and game development.

Some popular Japanese video games include:
- Super Mario Bros
- Space Invaders
- Pac-Man
- The Legend of Zelda
- Sonic the Hedgehog

CARS AND MOTORBIKES

Although China produces the most cars in the world, Japan is close behind in second place. Have you heard of Honda, Toyota, or Nissan? These are all Japanese car manufacturing companies that sell cars all around the world. Japan is also home to several motorbike manufacturers, including Kawasaki, Suzuki, and Yamaha. These are very popular motorbikes and are used as racing bikes in many countries.

A YAMAHA MOTORBIKE

JAPAN PRODUCES MORE THAN SEVEN MILLION CARS EVERY YEAR!

THESE ARE SOME EXAMPLES OF HONDA, TOYOTA, AND NISSAN CARS.

ROBOTS

As well as making cars, Honda does a lot of research on robots. One Honda robot is ASIMO, a robot that can talk to humans, walk up and down stairs, dance, and even help with carrying things. Honda calls ASIMO "the world's most advanced humanoid robot." This means that Honda believes ASIMO is the most lifelike robot in the world. ASIMO is 4 feet 3 inches (130 cm) tall, weighs 119 pounds (54 kg), and can be controlled by a computer, a wireless controller, or by voice commands.

ONE DAY, ASIMO WILL HELP IN HOMES AROUND THE WORLD!

So, what is manga?

Cool!

Manga is a Japanese comic book style that has been around since the 12th century!

....

Here's a manga comic for you to read.

But it doesn't make any sense!

That's because you read manga from right to left, not left to right!

Oh, I understand!

Is manga popular in Japan?

Yes, very! One manga comic book sold over two million copies in one year!

Wow!

Is manga the same as anime?

No, anime is like manga, but on TV. There are lots of anime cartoons and films in Japan, and some have gained popularity all over the world, like Pokémon.

Are manga and anime important to Japanese culture?

Yes, they are a big part of Japanese culture. Manga has influenced comics around the world, and people everywhere are interested in manga and anime.

KARAOKE

LET'S HAVE A SING-ALONG!

Unlike tea, toilet paper, and toothbrushes, karaoke is still quite a new invention. Daisuke Inoue invented the karaoke machine in Japan in 1971, and it was a great success. At first, karaoke machines were only in bars and restaurants, but eventually they were used in homes across Asia and the rest of the world. Karaoke machines were so popular that companies such as Nintendo and Sony released karaoke-based video games for consoles. Karaoke Revolution is a karaoke game, and Rock Band involves playing instruments and singing into a microphone.

KARAOKE (カラオケ) IS A JAPANESE WORD THAT MEANS "EMPTY ORCHESTRA."

HOW DO KARAOKE MACHINES WORK?

Karaoke machines are made up of a music player, a microphone, a screen, and a speaker. They play songs without any singing—this is called instrumental music. The words, or lyrics, to the song appear on a screen, and the person reads the lyrics and sings along to the music into the microphone. Karaoke songs are usually performed in front of an audience of friends, family, and strangers.

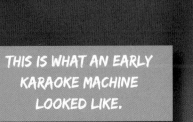

THIS IS WHAT AN EARLY KARAOKE MACHINE LOOKED LIKE.

ROBOTICS AND TECHNOLOGY

VIRTUAL SUPERMARKETS

South Korea is incredibly advanced in terms of technology. Around 80% of South Koreans own a smartphone, compared to around 70% of Americans!

Have you ever heard of a virtual supermarket? They exist in South Korea and allow people to shop using their smartphones!

First, you download an app onto your smartphone. This lets you scan **QR codes** underneath the pictures of the food you want to buy.

After you have scanned the QR code, you can choose where and when you would like your food delivered.

THIS IS HOW YOU SCAN A QR CODE.

SHOPPING IN TRADITIONAL SUPERMARKETS MAY BECOME A THING OF THE PAST IN SOUTH KOREA!

Virtual supermarkets are so successful in South Korea because people from South Korea work very long hours. In fact, South Korea has the third-longest working hours in the world! Ordering their food deliveries in subway stations on the way to work is more convenient and saves time.

ROBOTS

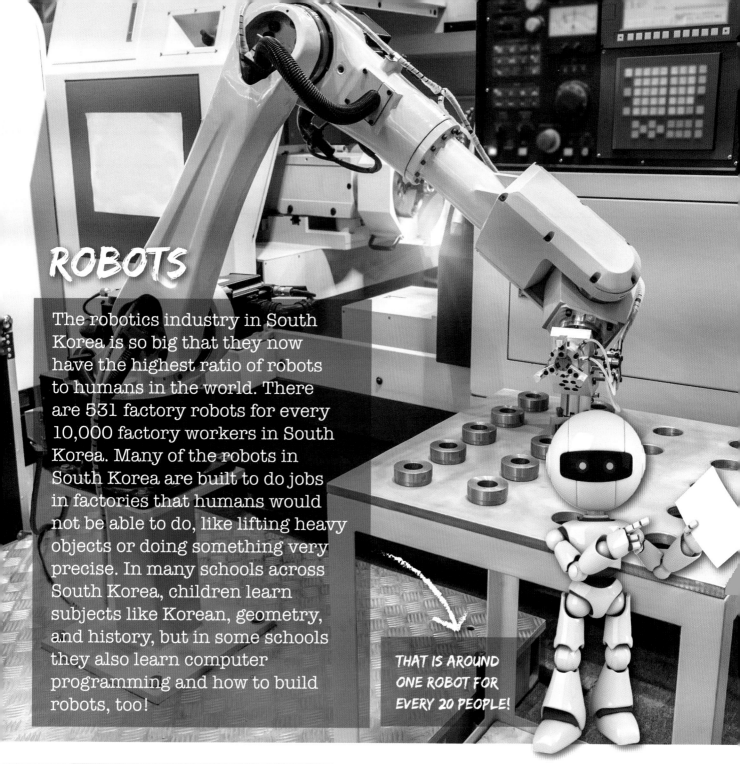

The robotics industry in South Korea is so big that they now have the highest ratio of robots to humans in the world. There are 531 factory robots for every 10,000 factory workers in South Korea. Many of the robots in South Korea are built to do jobs in factories that humans would not be able to do, like lifting heavy objects or doing something very precise. In many schools across South Korea, children learn subjects like Korean, geometry, and history, but in some schools they also learn computer programming and how to build robots, too!

THAT IS AROUND ONE ROBOT FOR EVERY 20 PEOPLE!

Just like Japan's Honda ASIMO robot, South Korea is moving more towards using robots in everyday life at home. Some schools in South Korea want to introduce robot teachers into their classrooms that might even be able to teach English!

WHAT DO YOU THINK ABOUT ROBOT TEACHERS? ARE THEY A GOOD IDEA? WHY OR WHY NOT?

CASE STUDY: SAMSUNG

Samsung was founded in 1938 by a man called Lee Byung-chul. It is South Korea's most well-known company. In the beginning, Samsung sold dried fish, vegetables, and fruit to cities in Asia. Lee Byung-chul soon earned enough money to buy more buildings and machines, and his company continued to grow from there. Samsung now sells a wide range of electrical products including smartphones, tablets, laptops, and televisions. You can even buy Samsung washing machines and dishwashers!

THIS IS WHAT SAMSUNG'S LOGO LOOKS LIKE.

DO YOU RECOGNIZE ANY OF THESE SAMSUNG PRODUCTS?

Did you know Samsung owns a hospital in South Korea? It is called the Samsung Medical Centre.

THIS IS KANGBUK SAMSUNG HOSPITAL, PART OF THE SAMSUNG MEDICAL CENTRE IN SOUTH KOREA.

TELEVISIONS

It may be difficult to imagine, but many years ago, color television did not exist. There were no LCD screens or HD quality pictures – all televisions were in black and white.
In 1976, Samsung produced one million black-and-white televisions. Only one year later in 1977, they started selling color televisions.

THIS IS AN OLD BLACK-AND-WHITE TELEVISION.

People still buy Samsung televisions today. In fact, Samsung is one of the biggest companies in the world that makes and sells televisions. Of all the money that South Korea makes, 20% comes from Samsung! This shows how important Samsung is to South Korea.

FOR EVERY $5 THAT SOUTH KOREA MAKES, $1 IS FROM SAMSUNG!

K-POP

WHAT IS K-POP?

K-Pop is an **abbreviation** of "Korean pop" or "Korean popular music." It is a **genre** of music and is a mixture of electronic, hip hop, pop, rock, and R&B sounds. The first K-Pop music bands began appearing in the 1990s, and the genre is now very popular in South Korea, Asia, and across the world.

SOME COMMON INSTRUMENTS USED IN K-POP MUSIC ARE GUITARS, SYNTHESIZERS, DRUMS, AND KEYBOARDS.

THIS IS A K-POP BAND CALLED AZIATIX.

K-POP SINGER PSY AND HIS SONG, "GANGNAM STYLE," WERE VERY POPULAR IN THE US.

One reason that K-Pop is popular around the world is because K-Pop bands include English words and phrases in their songs. Eighty million people speak Korean, but over 1 **billion** people speak English—that is a lot more people! This means that English-speaking people can understand and enjoy the music, too.

THIS IS A SYNTHESIZER.

THE CULTURE OF K-POP

All countries have a culture, which is a mix of values, traditions, and ways of life. K-Pop can be thought of as a small culture in itself. This is because K-Pop fans all listen to similar music and share the same interests in K-Pop fashion and style. Sharing a culture with people from around the world has become easier with use of the Internet. Music fans can share music and communicate with each other online—it is even possible to watch videos of your favorite K-pop bands.

SIXTY NEW BANDS COME FROM SOUTH KOREA EVERY YEAR!

Repetitive dance routines and lyrics, exciting backdrops, and brightly colored clothing make K-Pop performances and concerts memorable. This means that people can remember the bands and the songs more easily.

BIG FANS OF K-POP CAN JOIN CLUBS CALLED FANDOMS. YOU PAY A MEMBERSHIP PRICE AND GET SENT A MEMBERSHIP CARD AND MERCHANDISE.

K-POP FANS ALL OVER THE WORLD SHARE THIS CULTURE.

THE POSTAL SYSTEM

Around 800 years ago, the Mongolians had a very large empire that spread from western Russia all the way to China. The Mongol Empire was HUGE, and messages often had to be sent to traveling armies hundreds of miles away. This was many years before text messages or emails, so how did the Mongolians send messages quickly?

YAM

Yam, or Örtöö in Mongolian, was a way for Mongolian messengers to travel faster and send messages more quickly. Yam was a route across Mongolia that had postal stations every few miles. These postal stations had spare horses, food, and shelter. Mongolian messengers could use Yam like a relay race.

- The first messenger would run to the first station and give the message to the second messenger.
- The first messenger could rest while the second messenger ran to the second station.
- The second messenger gives the message to the third messenger, and so on.

The Mongolian postal system inspired modern postal systems all over the world.

INSTEAD OF PASSING A BATON, MONGOLIAN MESSENGERS PASSED MESSAGES.

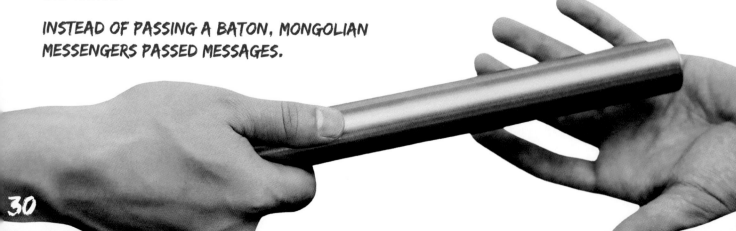

GLOSSARY

abbreviation   a shortened form of a word

aromatic   something that smells sweet, or like perfume

billion   one thousand million

calligraphy   the art of beautiful handwriting

characters   written letters or symbols

chemical   substances that are usually produced artificially by scientists

efficient   getting the most out of something in the best way possible

emperors   the male rulers in charge of an empire

enamel   the covering on teeth that protects them from food and drink

feng shui   creating peace in a room by placing objects in specific places

genre   a particular type, or sort, of something

hemispheres   sections of the Earth, either Northern, Southern, Eastern or Western

hog's hair   hair from a hog, an animal that is similar to a pig

imperial family   the family of a ruling emperor

magnetic field   a magnetic force around the world that has a north and a south

meditation   a peaceful and reflective form of relaxing

merchandise   branded products that promote pop groups, movies, and other media

orienteering   a cross-country race where people use a map and compass to find their way

philosophy   the study of the nature of knowledge, reality, and existence

profession   a job that needs special training

QR codes   symbols made of black and white squares that can be read by a scanner

Shamanism   a religion based on the belief in supernatural spirits

Shintoism   a religion whose followers worship nature and ancestors

synthesizer   a machine that can imitate musical sounds and other noises

Taoism   a religious system that teaches the simplicity of life

INDEX